Gifted for a Purpose

Aidan Browne

Published by Ursula Sanzie, 2024.

GIFTED FOR A PURPOSE

First edition. November 17, 2024.

ISBN: 979-8230230533

Written by Aidan Browne.

Table of Contents

Gifted for a Purpose

Unlocking Your Divine Potential

Aidan Browne

About the Author

Aidan Browne is an enthusiastic educator, orator, and author who is committed to assisting individuals in uncovering and utilizing their divinely endowed spiritual abilities. Aidan has devoted years of research, teaching, and counseling people on their spiritual journeys because he has a passion for ministry and a strong love for the Bible. His work is motivated by his passion to see individuals discover their purpose, deepen their religion, and have a positive impact on their communities.

Through a unique combination of biblical insight and useful tools, Aidan's approach empowers readers to recognize their spiritual strengths and put them into practice. In his writing, he exhorts believers to walk fearlessly in their calling, demonstrating his enthusiasm for mentoring, community building, and personal development.

Introduction

Have you ever felt that you're destined for something more—a life filled with purpose, fulfilment, and divine significance? This desire is no accident; it has been intricately woven into your very being by God. He has designed you with a unique purpose, and one of the most powerful ways He equips you to fulfil that purpose is through the spiritual gifts He has placed within you.

Scripture teaches us that as followers of Christ, we are not only forgiven and saved—we are also empowered and equipped. The Apostle Paul reminds us, *"There are different kinds of gifts, but the same Spirit distributes them. There are different kinds of service, but the same Lord. There are different kinds of working, but in all of them and everyone it is the same God at work" (1 Corinthians 12:4-6, NIV)*. Each of us has been uniquely gifted, and these gifts are not random. They have been given for a divine purpose: strengthening the Body of Christ and advancing His kingdom on earth.

Spiritual gifts are supernatural abilities bestowed by the Holy Spirit on every believer. Unlike talents or skills, which may align with our natural abilities, spiritual gifts are divinely granted to build up the Church and accomplish God's purposes. As Paul writes in *1 Corinthians 12:7, "Now to each one the manifestation of the Spirit is given for the common good."* These gifts are not for personal benefit or self-promotion. Instead, they are meant to serve others, glorify God, and advance His mission.

Each spiritual gift serves a distinct and divine purpose. Whether it is the gift of teaching, leadership, mercy, or prophecy, all are essential in advancing God's kingdom. Paul illustrates this beautifully in Romans 12:4-6: *"For just as each of us has one body with many members, and these members do not all have the same function, so in Christ we, though many, form one body, and each member belongs to all the others. We have different gifts, according to the grace given to each of us."*

The metaphor of the Church as a body is powerful. Just as the human body relies on every part to function effectively, so does the Church—the Body of Christ—depend on the gifts of every believer. When we activate and use our spiritual gifts, we contribute to the Church's vitality, growth, and mission. However, when we neglect or withhold our gifts, the Body of Christ is weakened.

The Importance of Discovering and Activating Your Gifts

Recognizing that you possess spiritual gifts is one aspect, but uncovering them and applying them is another challenge altogether. Many Christians navigate through life unaware of the gifts bestowed upon them by God, while others are aware but struggle to put them into action due to fears, self-doubt, or a lack of clarity.

Ephesians 4:11-12 reminds us that these gifts are given *"to equip his people for works of service, so that the body of Christ may be built up until we all reach unity in the faith and in the knowledge of the Son of God and become mature, attaining to the whole measure of the fullness of Christ."* God desires for us to be fully equipped, empowered, and actively engaged in His work. By uncovering and activating our spiritual gifts, we align ourselves with His divine purpose for our lives.

The message of this book is clear: you are gifted for a purpose. Whether you're new to your faith or have been walking with Christ for many years, God has placed unique gifts within you—gifts that are meant to be discovered, nurtured, and used. These gifts are not optional; they are vital to living a fulfilling and impactful Christian life.

Embarking on the journey to uncover and activate your spiritual gifts will not only deepen your relationship with God but also empower you to positively impact the lives of others. Throughout this guide, you'll find biblical wisdom, practical tools, and real-life stories designed to inspire and equip you to take the next step in your spiritual journey.

Paul's words to Timothy in 2 Timothy 1:6 are also a personal call to you*: "Fan into flame the gift of God, which is in you."* Whether your gift has been lying dormant or is only partially activated, now is the time to reignite it, step into the fullness of who God created you to be, and live a life that brings glory to Him.

In this book, we will journey together through ten essential areas that will guide you in discovering, understanding, and activating your spiritual gifts. Along the way, you will:

Gain a deep understanding of the biblical foundation for spiritual gifts, their purpose, and their significance in your life.

Explore the variety of gifts described in Scripture, including those mentioned in 1 Corinthians 12, Romans 12, and Ephesians 4.

Be inspired by personal testimonies of individuals who have discovered and activated their gifts, transforming not only their own lives but also their communities.

Engage in practical exercises and reflection questions designed to help you recognize and identify your unique gifts.

Learn how to overcome common obstacles like fear, self-doubt, and comparison that often hold believers back from fully utilizing their gifts.

Build a supportive community by finding mentors and friends who will encourage and help you grow in your gifting.

Discover how to integrate your gifts into all aspects of your life, not just within the church but in your work, relationships, and daily interactions.

Maintain spiritual vitality by staying connected to God, ensuring your gifts continue to grow and bear lasting fruit.

Each chapter will not only provide biblical insights but also offer practical steps you can immediately apply. At the end of every chapter, you'll find reflection questions and action steps to help you put what you've learned into practice. By the end of this journey, you will be fully equipped to confidently step into your God-given purpose, using the gifts He has entrusted to you.

As we embark on this journey together, I encourage you to take a moment to pray. Ask God to open your heart and mind as you seek to discover and understand the spiritual gifts He has placed within you. Pray for the Holy Spirit to reveal your gifts, remove any barriers that may be holding you back, and empower you to boldly walk in your calling.

In the words of 1 Peter 4:10 (NIV), *"Each of you should use whatever gift you have received to serve others, as faithful stewards of God's grace in its various forms."* This is your opportunity to embrace the gifts God has given you, to live a life that is true to His calling, and to make a lasting impact on His kingdom.

Let's begin this exciting journey together—discovering the gifts God has entrusted to you and unlocking the divine purpose He has for your life.

Chapter 1

The Divine Blueprint

What Are Spiritual Gifts?

Have you ever questioned what it truly means to be spiritually gifted? Many Christians are familiar with the term "spiritual gifts," yet few fully understand what these gifts entail, why they are significant, and how they fit into God's greater plan for His Church. In this chapter, we will delve into the biblical foundation of spiritual gifts, uncover their divine purpose, and explore how they function in the life of every believer. This understanding is key to recognizing not only what God has entrusted to us but also how we are called to use these gifts for His glory and the good of others.

The Source of Spiritual Gifts

Spiritual gifts are not the same as talents or learned skills; they are supernatural abilities given by the Holy Spirit to every believer. These gifts are not something we earn or deserve but are distributed by God according to His sovereign will and purpose.

The Apostle Paul explains this in 1 Corinthians 12:4-6 (NIV): *"There are different kinds of gifts, but the same Spirit distributes them. There are different kinds of service, but the same Lord. There are different kinds of working, but in all of them and everyone it is the same God at work."* From this passage, we can draw three important insights:

1. Gifts are diverse – There are many types of spiritual gifts, each created to fulfil a specific purpose.
2. Gifts are given by the Holy Spirit – These are not natural talents, but supernatural abilities empowered by God.
3. Gifts are for the common good – Spiritual gifts are given to serve others and advance God's kingdom.

These truths remind us that spiritual gifts are not merely for our benefit; they are essential to God's plan for the Church and the world. Whether your gift is teaching, serving, leadership, or prophecy, it has been given to you by God for a meaningful purpose.

Biblical Foundation for Spiritual Gifts

The New Testament provides several key passages that give us a clear understanding of spiritual gifts and how they function. The most detailed list of spiritual gifts is found in 1 Corinthians 12:7-11:

"Now to each one, the manifestation of the Spirit is given for the common good. To one there is given through the Spirit a message of wisdom, to another a message of knowledge through the same Spirit, to another faith by the same Spirit, to another gift of healing by that one Spirit, to another miraculous power, to another prophecy, to another distinguishing between spirits, to another speaking in different kinds of tongues, and to still another the interpretation of tongues. All these are the work of the same Spirit, and he distributes them to each one, just as he determines."

In this passage, Paul emphasizes that spiritual gifts are not self-generated but are manifestations of the Holy Spirit working through believers. They are given "for the common good"—to bless others, strengthen the Church, and demonstrate God's power.

Paul also writes about spiritual gifts in Romans 12:6-8 (NIV):

"We have different gifts, according to the grace given to each of us. If your gift is prophesying, then prophesy by your faith; if it is serving, then serve; if it is teaching, then teach; if it is to encourage, then give encouragement; if it is giving, then give generously; if it is to lead, do it diligently; if it is to show mercy, do it cheerfully."

In this passage, Paul lists a variety of gifts and underscores the importance of using them. Notice his focus on action: prophesy, serve, teach, encourage, give, lead, and show mercy. The message is clear—whatever gift you have, it is meant to be actively used for the benefit of others.

Finally, in Ephesians 4:11-12 (NIV), Paul explains the purpose of ministry gifts:

"So Christ himself gave the apostles, the prophets, the evangelists, the pastors and teachers, to equip his people for works of service, so that the body of Christ may be built up."

These ministry gifts are designed to equip believers for service, with the ultimate goal of building up the Church. Whether your role is more visible, like teaching, or more behind-the-scenes, like serving, your gift is essential for the health and growth of the Body of Christ. Each believer's contribution strengthens the Church and helps fulfil God's purposes.

The Purpose of Spiritual Gifts

What is the purpose of spiritual gifts? They are not given for personal enjoyment, self-promotion, or to create a sense of importance. Instead, they serve three primary purposes that align with God's greater plan:

1. To Build Up the Body of Christ

Paul uses the metaphor of a physical body to describe the Church, emphasizing that each member has a crucial role. In 1 Corinthians 12:12-14 (NIV), he writes:

"Just as a body, though one, has many parts, but all its many parts form one body, so it is with Christ. For we were all baptized by one Spirit to form one body—whether Jews or Gentiles, slave or free—and we were all given the one Spirit to drink. Even so, the body is not made up of one part but of many."

Every believer is part of this body, and every gift is essential. Just as the physical body needs hands, feet, eyes, and ears to function, the Church needs a variety of spiritual gifts to work properly. Each gift supports and strengthens the whole, contributing to the Church's mission and spiritual growth.

2. To Glorify God

Spiritual gifts reflect God's character and His power at work in the world. When we use our gifts, we give glory to the One who gave them. 1 Peter 4:10-11 (NIV) encourages believers in this way:

"Each of you should use whatever gift you have received to serve others, as faithful stewards of God's grace in its various forms. If anyone speaks, they should do so as one who speaks the very words of God; if anyone serves, they should do so with the strength God provides, so that in all things God may be praised through Jesus Christ."

By using our gifts, we point others to God, acknowledging that the power and ability come from Him. This brings glory to God, as others see His grace and strength manifested through our service.

3. To Serve Others

The gifts are not for personal gain but to serve the needs of others. 1 Corinthians 12:7 (NIV) reminds us that the gifts are given *"for the common good."* Whether you are leading, teaching, encouraging, or showing mercy, your spiritual gift is meant to bless and uplift those around you. The gifts are designed to build community, encourage faith, and foster unity within the Church.

In summary, spiritual gifts are meant to build up the Church, glorify God, and serve others. When we recognize and use these gifts with the right heart, we not only fulfil God's purpose for our lives but also contribute to the growth and health of the Body of Christ.

Practical Examples

Using Spiritual Gifts in Everyday Life

Imagine possessing the gift of encouragement. While it may appear less prominent compared to more visible gifts like prophecy, its impact is profoundly significant. Consider a man in your church who is navigating a tough season in his life. You feel prompted by the Holy Spirit to share words of life and hope with him. Those words become a pivotal moment for him, helping him regain faith and find renewed strength in God. In that instance, you have activated your gift and fulfilled a portion of your God-given purpose.

Now, think of someone with the gift of administration. They may not aspire to stand on stage or preach, but they excel at organizing and coordinating events. Their diligent work behind the scenes ensures the church runs smoothly, allowing others to effectively utilize their gifts. Without this individual's contribution, the ministry's impact would diminish significantly.

In both examples, these believers are using their gifts to glorify God and edify the Body of Christ. Whether visible or hidden, every gift plays an essential role. Each contribution, no matter how small it may seem, is vital to the overall mission and health of the Church. This demonstrates that every believer's gift, regardless of its visibility, holds immense value in advancing God's kingdom and supporting the community of faith.

The Call to Use Your Gifts

Discovering your spiritual gift is just the beginning of an exciting journey. Paul's encouragement to Timothy in 2 Timothy 1:6 (NIV) serves as a reminder for us today: *"Fan into flame the gift of God, which is in you."* Just like a fire requires stoking to burn brightly, your spiritual gifts need to be nurtured, developed, and consistently exercised to flourish.

You might find yourself feeling uncertain about what your specific gift is, or perhaps you are aware of it but have hesitated to put it into action. It's important to remember that your gift is a divine endowment from God, intended for His glory and the benefit of others. As you continue through this book, you will encounter various tools and practical exercises designed to assist you in discovering, developing, and activating the gifts God has placed within you.

Embrace this opportunity to grow and learn. By actively engaging with your gifts, you can unlock your potential and step confidently into the role God has for you in His kingdom. The journey of activating your gifts is not only transformative for you but can also profoundly impact those around you, as you contribute to the life of the Church and the advancement of God's mission.

• • • •

Reflection Questions:

THESE REFLECTION QUESTIONS are great for helping individuals identify and engage with their spiritual gifts. Here's how one might approach answering each question:

- What do you believe are the spiritual gifts God has given you?

Take a moment to reflect on the abilities and passions that seem to align with God's purpose in your life. Consider gifts such as encouragement, teaching, leadership, serving, mercy, or hospitality. You might also think about instances where you felt particularly energized or fulfilled while helping others, as these experiences can often reveal your spiritual gifts.

In what areas of your life have you seen evidence of these gifts at work?

Look back at moments in your life when you felt effective or impactful in your interactions with others. Perhaps you've had the opportunity to mentor someone and see them grow in their faith. Or maybe you've organized events that brought people together and strengthened community bonds. Recognizing these moments can affirm the gifts God has bestowed upon you and encourage you to continue using them.

- How can you begin using your gifts to serve others and glorify God?

  Think about practical steps you can take to activate your gifts. This could involve volunteering in your church, leading a small group, or simply reaching out to someone in need of encouragement. You might also consider sharing your journey with trusted friends or mentors who can help you identify opportunities to use your gifts. Remember, no act of service is too small; every contribution can bring glory to God and make a difference in the lives of others.

By answering these questions, you can gain clarity on your spiritual gifts and how to actively engage them in your daily life.

Action Step

Take time this week to pray, inviting the Holy Spirit to reveal any spiritual gifts you may not yet recognize. Reflect on how you can utilize these gifts within your church, workplace, or community.

This chapter establishes the biblical groundwork for understanding spiritual gifts and prepares you for the journey ahead. As we progress, you will discover how to identify your gifts and learn how to overcome the challenges that frequently hinder believers from activating their God-given abilities.

Chapter 2

The Journey of Discovery

If you've ever questioned what specific gifts God has bestowed upon you, you're not alone. Many Christians yearn to serve God and His Church but often feel unsure about how they can uniquely contribute. Identifying your spiritual gifts involves a journey of self-discovery, reflection, and seeking God's guidance. In this chapter, we will explore the various types of spiritual gifts outlined in Scripture and provide practical steps to help you discern which gifts may belong to you.

Biblical Overview of Spiritual Gifts

The Bible categorizes several types of spiritual gifts in three primary passages: 1 Corinthians 12:4-11, Romans 12:6-8, and Ephesians 4:11. These gifts can be grouped into three main categories: motivational gifts, ministry gifts, and manifestation gifts. Understanding these distinctions can help you recognize how God might be working through you.

1. Motivational Gifts (Romans 12:6-8)

In Romans 12:6-8 (NIV), Paul states, *"We have different gifts, according to the grace given to each of us. If your gift is prophesying, then prophesy by your faith; if it is serving, then serve; if it is teaching, then teach; if it is to encourage, then give encouragement; if it is giving, then give generously; if it is to lead, do it diligently; if it is to show mercy, do it cheerfully."*

These gifts are often called motivational gifts because they reflect your natural inclinations in serving God and others. They shape how you view the world and approach ministry:

- Prophecy: Speaking truth in a way that encourages and challenges others to align with God's will.
- Serving: Offering practical assistance and meeting physical needs.
- Teaching: Clarifying and explaining biblical truths to foster knowledge and understanding.
- Encouraging (Exhortation): Uplifting others through words of affirmation and motivation.
- Giving: Generously sharing resources, time, and finances to further God's kingdom.
- Leading: Providing vision and direction to inspire and organize others.

- Showing Mercy: Extending compassion and care to those who are suffering or in need.

2. Ministry Gifts (Ephesians 4:11)

In Ephesians 4:11-12 (NIV), Paul explains, *"So Christ himself gave the apostles, the prophets, the evangelists, the pastors, and teachers, to equip his people for works of service, so that the body of Christ may be built up."*

These gifts, often referred to as ministry gifts, focus on leadership and equipping others within the Church:

- Apostles: Pioneers who plant churches, oversee ministries, and establish new works for the kingdom.

- Prophets: Individuals who receive and convey God's will, often emphasizing repentance or encouraging faithfulness.

- Evangelists: Believers passionate about sharing the Gospel and leading others to faith in Christ.

- Pastors: Shepherds who care for the spiritual well-being of a congregation, nurturing, counselling, and guiding believers.

- Teachers: Those capable of explaining and applying God's Word in ways that foster growth in faith.

3. Manifestation Gifts (1 Corinthians 12:4-11)

Lastly, 1 Corinthians 12:7-11 (NIV) presents what are known as manifestation gifts, showcasing the supernatural workings of the Holy Spirit:

- Wisdom: Supernatural insight into God's plans or purposes in specific situations.

- Knowledge: A profound, God-given understanding of spiritual truths or facts that are not naturally known.

- Faith: Extraordinary confidence in God's ability to accomplish the impossible.

• Healing: The ability to bring about physical, emotional, or spiritual healing through prayer.

• Miraculous Powers: Performing signs and wonders that reveal God's power.

• Prophecy: Delivering a message from God, whether for the present or future, to encourage or correct.

• Distinguishing between Spirits: The ability to discern spiritual influences, whether they come from God, humanity, or the enemy.

• Tongues: Speaking in an unknown language inspired by the Holy Spirit.

• Interpretation of Tongues: The ability to interpret what has been spoken in tongues for the edification of the Church.

Practical Tools for Identifying Your Gifts

• • • •

1. REFLECT ON YOUR Passion and Joy

A significant indicator of your spiritual gifts lies in your passions and the joy you experience while serving. God often places specific burdens on our hearts for certain ministries or services that align with the gifts He has given us. Consider the following questions:

- What activities in ministry bring me the most joy?
- Where do I feel most energized while serving others?
- When do I sense God's pleasure and feel His presence working through me?

For instance, if you feel fulfilled when encouraging others, you may possess the gift of exhortation. If teaching God's Word fills you with joy and purpose, then your gift could be teaching.

2. Seek Feedback from Others

Often, those around us—friends, family, pastors, and fellow believers—can identify our gifts more clearly than we can ourselves. Approach those who know you well and ask:

- Where have you seen God use me in significant ways?
- What strengths do you notice in me when I serve in the church or community?
- Have you ever observed me operating in a spiritual gift, even if I didn't recognize it?

Other believers can help affirm the gifts you may hesitate to acknowledge or be unaware of. Their insights can be invaluable in your discovery journey.

3. Try Different Areas of Ministry

Sometimes, the best way to uncover your gifts is through hands-on experience. If you're uncertain about your gifts, consider serving in various ministry areas. Whether it's teaching a Sunday school class, volunteering at a homeless outreach, or assisting in organizing a church event, these experiences allow you to explore where your gifts may lie.

As you serve, take note of how God works through you and where you feel most effective. You might discover a talent for administration if you excel at organizing events, or you may realize you have a special gift for mercy as you interact with those in need.

4. Spiritual Gifts Assessment

Another useful tool is a spiritual gifts assessment. These assessments help you reflect on your strengths, experiences, and areas of ministry that resonate with you. Typically, they consist of a series of questions that highlight tendencies or preferences related to specific gifts.

While these assessments are not definitive, they can provide valuable insights and guide you toward recognizing your gifts. Many churches and online resources offer free spiritual gift assessments that you can complete as part of your exploration.

5. Prayer and Discernment

Ultimately, discovering your spiritual gifts is a spiritual process that requires prayer and discernment. As you seek to identify your gifts, ask God to reveal them to you. James 1:5 (NIV) encourages us to seek wisdom: *"If any of you lacks wisdom, you should ask God, who gives generously to all without finding fault, and it will be given to you."*

Spend time in prayer, asking the Holy Spirit for guidance. Be patient; discovering your gifts may take time, and trust that God will reveal them as you seek Him.

Personal Example
Discovering the Gift of Teaching

Take the story of Sarah, a woman who always cherished reading and discussing the Bible with others but never thought of herself as a teacher. She believed that teaching was a role meant for pastors or those with seminary training. However, her pastor encouraged her to lead a small Bible study group. Initially, Sarah felt anxious about this new responsibility, but as she prepared each lesson, she discovered how much she loved breaking down Scripture and explaining it to others.

The members of her group frequently expressed their appreciation for her clarity and the insights they gained from her teachings. Through this experience, Sarah uncovered her gift of teaching. What began as a hesitant step of faith blossomed into a flourishing ministry, where she now teaches regularly and leads multiple Bible study groups.

Obstacles to Recognizing Your Gifts

Even as we begin to identify our spiritual gifts, several challenges can hinder us from fully acknowledging or embracing them:

1. Comparison: It's natural to compare your gifts with those of others, leading you to believe that your gifts are less valuable or less significant. However, it's important to remember that every gift is essential to the Body of Christ, whether it involves teaching, serving, or showing mercy. As 1 Corinthians 12:18 (NIV) reminds us, "*God has placed the parts in the body, every one of them, just as he wanted them to be.*"

2. Fear: You might feel apprehensive about stepping into a new role or using your gift in public settings. Remember, God equips those He calls. Pray for the courage to move forward and take small, obedient steps.

3. Insecurity: Many of us struggle with feelings of unworthiness or inadequacy when it comes to using the gifts God has entrusted to us. It's crucial to remember that it's not about your abilities, but about God's power working through you. Philippians 4:13 (NIV) assures us, "I can do all this through him who gives me strength."

Reflection Questions:

- Which activities or ministries have brought you the greatest joy or fulfilment in the past?
- What gifts have others recognized in you, and how have you witnessed God working through you in those areas?
- Are there any barriers, such as fear or insecurity that are preventing you from utilizing your gifts?

Action Step:

This week, dedicate some time to pray and reflect on your spiritual gifts. If you haven't done so already, consider taking a spiritual gifts assessment or exploring a new area of ministry. Remain open to where God may guide you.

In this chapter, we have examined the biblical foundation for spiritual gifts and practical steps for identifying your own. In the next chapter, we will delve deeper into how to cultivate and activate these gifts for God's glory and the benefit of others.

Chapter 3

Nurturing and Activating Your Spiritual Gifts

Now that you've begun identifying your spiritual gifts, the next step is to nurture and activate them. Spiritual gifts are like seeds planted within you—they require care, attention, and nourishment to flourish. While God provides the gifts, we must develop and utilize them effectively. In this chapter, we'll explore practical ways to nurture your gifts and take bold steps to activate them in your life and ministry.

The Process of Nurturing Your Spiritual Gifts

Just as any skill or talent needs practice and refinement, spiritual gifts also require intentional nurturing. Paul's advice to Timothy serves as a powerful reminder for all believers: *"For this reason, I remind you to fan into flame the gift of God, which is in you through the laying on of my hands"* (2 Timothy 1:6, NIV).

Paul encourages Timothy not to let his gift lie dormant but to "fan into flame" the gift of God. This imagery of a flame suggests that our gifts must be continually tended to, nurtured, and encouraged to grow. Here are some practical ways to cultivate your spiritual gifts:

1. Study and Seek Knowledge

Whatever gift God has bestowed upon you, developing a deeper understanding of how it operates is vital. If your gift is teaching, immerse yourself in studying Scripture and biblical interpretation. If your gift is mercy, learn more about serving others and understanding their emotional and spiritual needs.

The Bible encourages us to seek knowledge and wisdom as we grow in our spiritual journey. Proverbs 4:7 (NIV) states, *"The beginning of wisdom is this: Get wisdom. Though it cost all you have, get understanding."* Invest time in studying Scripture, attending workshops, reading Christian literature, and seeking mentors who can help you grow in your gift.

For instance, consider Anna, who discovered her gift of administration. She started by reading books on church organization and project management, attending leadership training sessions, and volunteering for increasingly complex responsibilities at her church. Through intentional learning, her gift became more effective in serving her church.

2. Pray for Guidance and Strength

Prayer is the cornerstone of spiritual growth. When it comes to nurturing your spiritual gifts, prayer is essential for seeking guidance, strength, and wisdom from God. Ask the Holy Spirit to help you grow in your gift, guide you to the right opportunities, and empower you to use your gifts effectively.

Jesus emphasized the importance of prayer when He said, *"Ask and it will be given to you; seek and you will find; knock and the door will be opened to you"* (Matthew 7:7, NIV). This promise extends to your spiritual gifts—ask God to help you fan your gifts into flame, and trust that He will provide the wisdom and opportunities needed to activate them.

3. Practice and Use Your Gifts

The best way to nurture your spiritual gifts is through active use. Like any skill, practice leads to improvement and confidence. Whether your gift is teaching, serving, leadership, or encouragement, find ways to practice your gift in your church, community, and daily life.

In Romans 12:6 (NIV), Paul writes, *"We have different gifts, according to the grace given to each of us. If your gift is prophesying, then prophesy by your faith."* In other words, whatever gift you possess, use it according to the grace and faith God has given you. This act of practice strengthens and refines your gift.

For example, if you believe you have the gift of teaching, begin small by leading a Bible study group or teaching a Sunday school class. If your gift is hospitality, invite people into your home and practice serving them. Don't wait for the perfect opportunity; start using your gifts where you are, allowing God to grow them over time.

4. Seek Feedback and Accountability

An essential aspect of nurturing your spiritual gifts is being open to feedback and accountability. Often, others can see areas for growth or improvement that we might overlook. Ask trusted friends, mentors, or church leaders to provide feedback on how you're using your gift. They can help identify strengths and suggest areas for further development.

Proverbs 27:17 (NIV) reminds us, *"As iron sharpens iron, so one person sharpens another."* We need others to help refine our gifts, just as they need us to encourage them in their spiritual growth. Be willing to receive constructive criticism and seek advice from those with more experience in ministry.

5. Step Out in Faith

One of the most important ways to nurture your spiritual gifts is to take bold steps of faith. Often, fear or uncertainty can hold us back from fully stepping into the gifts God has given us. We might wonder, "Am I equipped for this?" or "What if I fail?"

However, God calls us to trust Him and take steps of faith, even when we feel inadequate. Hebrews 11:6 (NIV) reminds us, *"And without faith, it is impossible to please God because anyone who comes to him must believe that he exists and that he rewards those who earnestly seek him."*

Faith involves taking risks and trusting that God will provide what is needed to fulfil His purpose. If you sense God leading you to use your gift in a new way—whether that's teaching, leading a ministry, or serving in a new capacity—trust Him to give you the strength and wisdom you need

Activating Your Spiritual Gifts in Ministry

Once you've begun nurturing your gifts, the next step is to activate them. Activation means using your gifts intentionally and regularly in ministry to bless others and build up the Body of Christ. But how do you transition from nurturing your gift privately to activating it in your church, community, or workplace?

1. Start Small and Be Faithful

You don't need a grand platform to activate your spiritual gifts. Many impactful ministries begin with small, faithful acts of service. Jesus said, *"Whoever can be trusted with very little can also be trusted with much"* (Luke 16:10, NIV).

Start by serving in a small capacity, whether that's volunteering at church, helping with a ministry team, or offering your gifts to those around you. As you are faithful in small things, God will open up greater opportunities for you to use your gifts.

2. Connect with a Ministry or Need

One of the most effective ways to activate your gifts is by connecting with a ministry or a need in your community. Look for areas where your gifts can serve a purpose. If you have the gift of mercy, consider volunteering with a homeless ministry or hospital outreach. If you have the gift of leadership, offer to help organize an event or lead a small group.

God often leads us to opportunities where our gifts can meet a need. By connecting with a ministry or need, you create space for God to work powerfully through your gifts.

3. Rely on the Holy Spirit

As you activate your gifts in ministry, remember that they are empowered by the Holy Spirit, not by your strength. Zechariah 4:6 (NIV) says, *"'Not by might nor by power, but by my Spirit,' says the Lord Almighty."*

Relying on the Holy Spirit means staying connected to God through prayer, listening for His guidance, and being sensitive to how He wants to use your gifts in each situation. The more you depend on the Holy Spirit, the more effective your gifts will be in building up the Body of Christ.

4. Keep Growing and Learning

Activation is not a one-time event; it's a continuous process of growth and learning. As you use your gifts in ministry, continue to seek God's guidance and look for opportunities to further develop your skills. Attend workshops, participate in leadership training, or join a group of like-minded individuals who are also growing in their gifts.

Philippians 1:6 (NIV) encourages us: *"Being confident of this, that he who began a good work in you will carry it on to completion until the day of Christ Jesus."* Trust that God will continue to grow and refine your gifts as you faithfully use them.

Personal Example
Stepping Out in Faith

Consider the story of Mark, who felt called to lead worship but had never sung or played an instrument in front of others. He knew God placed a desire in his heart to lead others in prayer, but fear and self-doubt held him back for years. One day, his pastor encouraged him to take a small step by leading worship for the youth group.

Though Mark felt nervous, he trusted God and took the step. The youth group responded enthusiastically, and over time, Mark's confidence grew. Now, he regularly leads worship at his church, and his ministry has blossomed. By stepping out in faith, Mark activated the gift God placed within him, transforming it into a powerful way to serve the Body of Christ.

Overcoming Challenges in Activation

As you seek to activate your gifts, you may face challenges. These can range from internal struggles like fear and doubt to external obstacles such as lack of opportunity or discouragement from others. However, overcoming these challenges is part of the journey, and God promises to be with you every step of the way.

1. Fear of Failure

A common challenge is the fear of failure. You might worry about making mistakes or not measuring up to others who seem more experienced or gifted. Remember, God's power is made perfect in weakness. 2 Corinthians 12:9 (NIV) says, *"But he said to me, 'My grace is sufficient for you, for my power is made perfect in weakness.'"*

2. Lack of Opportunity

Another challenge you might face is a lack of clear opportunities to use your gifts. If you find yourself in this situation, consider creating your opportunities. You could start a small group, volunteer to assist a ministry leader or offer your skills to a local organization. God can use your initiative to open doors you may not have previously considered.

3. Discouragement

Finally, discouragement from others can sometimes hinder the activation of your gifts. Perhaps someone has criticized your efforts or doubted your ability. In these moments, it's crucial to remember that your calling comes from God, not from people. Galatians 1:10 (NIV) reminds us, *"Am I now trying to win the approval of human beings, or God? Or am I trying to please people? If I were still trying to please people, I would not be a servant of Christ."*

Stay focused on God's purpose for you, and trust that He will provide the strength and encouragement you need to persevere.

Reflection Questions

- What steps can you take this week to begin cultivating your spiritual gifts?

- Are there any specific areas of ministry or community needs where your gifts could be activated?

- How can you rely more on the Holy Spirit as you seek to activate your gifts?

Action Step

This week, choose one practical way to activate your spiritual gift. Whether it's volunteering, leading a group, or offering your skills to others, take a step of faith and trust that God will work through you.

In this chapter, we've explored how to cultivate and activate your spiritual gifts through prayer, practice, and stepping out in faith. The next chapter will address some of the common obstacles to using your gifts and how you can overcome them with confidence and trust in God.

Chapter 4

Overcoming Obstacles and Challenges in Activating Your Spiritual Gifts

As you begin to discover, cultivate, and activate your spiritual gifts, you may face various obstacles. These challenges are part of the journey, but they can sometimes hinder you from fully stepping into the gifts God has given you. In this chapter, we will explore common obstacles such as fear, self-doubt, comparison, and external resistance. We will also discuss how you can overcome these challenges and walk confidently in your God-given purpose.

Fear and Insecurity

• • • •

ONE OF THE MOST SIGNIFICANT obstacles to activating spiritual gifts is fear. Many Christians feel anxious or inadequate when stepping out to use their gifts, afraid of making mistakes or failing to meet others' expectations. This fear can paralyze us, preventing us from using the very gifts God has entrusted to us.

Biblical Example: Moses' Fear

A powerful biblical example of overcoming fear is Moses. When God called Moses to lead the Israelites out of Egypt, Moses responded with fear and insecurity. He said, *"Who am I that I should go to Pharaoh and bring the Israelites out of Egypt?"* (Exodus 3:11, NIV). Moses felt inadequate for the task and even doubted his ability to speak effectively. Yet God reassured him, promising His presence and provision:

"Now go; I will help you speak and will teach you what to say." (Exodus 4:12, NIV)

Moses' story reminds us that our fears are no match for God's power. When God calls you to use your gifts, He will equip you for the task. He doesn't expect you to have all the answers or be perfect. Instead, He wants you to trust Him and take the first step.

Practical Tip: Prayer and Trust

If fear and insecurity are holding you back, bring these concerns to God in prayer. Ask Him for courage, and remind yourself that your strength comes from Him. Philippians 4:13 (NIV) says, *"I can do all this through him who gives me strength."* Trust that God will help you overcome your fears as you step out in faith.

Start small. If you're afraid of using your gift in a public setting, consider practicing it in a smaller, more comfortable environment. For example, if you have the gift of teaching but feel anxious about leading a large Bible study, begin by sharing insights with a close group of friends or mentoring one person. The more you use your gift, the more confident you will become.

Self-Doubt and Comparison

Another common obstacle is self-doubt. You may find yourself thinking, "Am I gifted in this area?" or "What if someone else is better than me?" Self-doubt often leads to comparison, where we measure our gifts against those of others. This can create feelings of inadequacy or envy, hindering our effectiveness.

Biblical Example: The Parable of the Talents

Jesus addressed the issue of comparison and self-doubt in the Parable of the Talents. In Matthew 25:14-30, a master gives his servants different amounts of talents (money) according to their ability. While two servants invest and multiply their talents, the third servant hides his talent out of fear, saying, *"I was afraid and went out and hid your gold in the ground."* (Matthew 25:25, NIV). This servant's fear and comparison to others led him to bury his gift rather than use it for God's purposes.

The lesson here is clear: God has given each of us gifts according to His purpose for our lives. He doesn't compare us to others, nor should we. Our responsibility is to use what we've been given, trusting that God has equipped us uniquely for the role He has assigned to us.

Practical Tip: Embrace Your Unique Calling

Instead of comparing yourself to others, focus on the unique gifts and calling that God has given you. Ephesians 2:10 (NIV) says, *"For we are God's handiwork, created in Christ Jesus to do good works, which God prepared in advance for us to do."* You are uniquely crafted by God for a specific purpose, and your gifts—no matter how different or small they may seem—are valuable in His eyes.

If you struggle with self-doubt, surround yourself with people who can encourage and affirm your gifts. Ask friends or mentors to give you feedback and affirm how they see God working in you. Sometimes, the encouragement of others helps us recognize what we might not see in ourselves.

External Opposition and Discouragement

It's not uncommon to face opposition or discouragement from external sources as you seek to activate your spiritual gifts. This may come from others who misunderstand or downplay your gifts, or from circumstances that make it difficult to serve in the way God has called you.

Biblical Example: Nehemiah's Opposition

Nehemiah faced significant external opposition as he sought to rebuild the walls of Jerusalem. His enemies mocked and ridiculed him, saying, *"What are those feeble Jews doing? Will they restore their wall?"* (Nehemiah 4:2, NIV). Despite the discouragement and threats, Nehemiah remained focused on the work God had given him, praying for strength and continuing the task with determination:

"The God of heaven will give us success. We his servants will start rebuilding." (Nehemiah 2:20, NIV)

Nehemiah's response is a powerful reminder that opposition should not deter us from using our gifts. When God gives us a purpose, we can trust that He will also give us the strength and perseverance to complete it, even when we face resistance.

Practical Tip: Persevere in Faith

If you encounter external opposition or discouragement, remember that God is greater than any obstacle you may face. Stay rooted in His Word and prayer, and ask Him for the strength to persevere. James 1:12 (NIV) encourages us, *"Blessed is the one who perseveres under trial because, having stood the test, that person will receive the crown of life that the Lord has promised to those who love him."*

Stay connected to a supportive community of believers who can encourage you and help you stay focused on God's call. When opposition comes, having a strong support system can make all the difference in maintaining your confidence and perseverance.

Lack of Opportunities or Resources

Sometimes the obstacle to activating your gifts isn't internal or relational but circumstantial. You may feel that there are no opportunities for you to use your gifts or that you lack the resources or platform needed to fulfil your calling.

Biblical Example: David's Preparation

Before David became king of Israel, he spent many years as a shepherd. Though it may have seemed like an insignificant role, God used this time to prepare David for future leadership. David's faithfulness in the small, seemingly mundane tasks was a crucial part of his preparation for the greater responsibilities ahead:

"Whoever can be trusted with very little can also be trusted with much." (Luke 16:10, NIV)

Just like David, you may be in a season where opportunities to use your gifts seem limited. However, God often uses these times to refine and prepare us for future ministry. Don't despise small beginnings; trust that God is working behind the scenes, preparing you for greater things.

Practical Tip: Create Opportunities

If you feel that there are no clear opportunities to use your gifts, consider creating your own. Start a small group, volunteer at a local charity, or offer your skills to those in need. Sometimes, stepping out in faith and serving in a less formal capacity opens doors for greater ministry opportunities later on.

Remember, God isn't waiting for you to find the perfect platform or resources. He's simply asking for your faithfulness in the present moment, trusting that He will provide everything you need.

Overcoming Internal and External Challenges with God's Help

No matter what obstacles you face—whether internal fears, external opposition, or circumstantial challenges—God is with you. He has given you your gifts for a purpose, and He will help you overcome every hindrance that comes your way.

Isaiah 41:10 (NIV) reminds us, *"So do not fear, for I am with you; do not be dismayed, for I am your God. I will strengthen you and help you; I will uphold you with my righteous right hand."*

Trust in God's promises, and remember that He is faithful to complete the good work He has started in you.

Reflection Questions:

- What internal obstacles, such as fear or self-doubt, are holding you back from using your gifts?
- How have you experienced external opposition or discouragement, and how can you persevere in faith?
- What opportunities—big or small—can you create to activate your spiritual gifts this week?

Action Step:

This week, identify one obstacle that has been holding you back from using your spiritual gifts. Take time to pray about this challenge, and ask God for the wisdom and strength to overcome it. Then, take a bold step to use your gifts, even if it feels small or risky.

In this chapter, we've explored the various challenges that can hinder us from using our spiritual gifts and how we can overcome them. The next chapter will focus on building a supportive community around you to nurture and encourage your spiritual growth

Chapter 5

Building a Supportive Community and Finding Mentors for Spiritual Growth

As you embark on the journey of discovering and activating your spiritual gifts, one of the most vital elements for success is building a supportive community. God designed us to live and grow in relationship with one another, and that includes growing in the gifts He has given us. A healthy community provides encouragement, accountability, and wisdom, and mentors help guide you through the process of spiritual development. In this chapter, we'll explore how to find the right people to support your journey, how to cultivate meaningful relationships, and the importance of having mentors in your life.

The Biblical Model of Community

Throughout Scripture, we see the importance of community for spiritual growth. The early church, described in the book of Acts, gives us a powerful example of believers coming together to support and encourage one another. Acts 2:42 (NIV) says, *"They devoted themselves to the apostles' teaching and fellowship, to the breaking of bread and prayer."* The early Christians understood that they needed one another to grow in their faith and to activate their spiritual gifts.

This model of community—teaching, fellowship, prayer, and shared life—reminds us that we cannot grow in isolation. We need to surround ourselves with people who share our faith and values, and who will support us as we discover and use our spiritual gifts.

Practical Example: A Small Group's Support

Consider the story of Sarah, who discovered her gift of teaching but was unsure how to use it. She joined a small group at her church, where the members encouraged her to lead a Bible study. With their support, Sarah began teaching weekly lessons, and over time, her confidence and abilities grew. The group provided constructive feedback, celebrated her progress, and prayed for her every step of the way. Without the support of that community, Sarah might never have had the courage to step into her gift.

Like Sarah, you may find that your spiritual gifts are best developed in the context of a small group or close-knit community where you can receive encouragement, feedback, and prayer.

The Role of Mentors in Spiritual Growth

In addition to a supportive community, having a mentor is essential for spiritual growth. A mentor is someone who has walked the path of faith ahead of you and can provide guidance, wisdom, and encouragement as you develop your spiritual gifts. Mentors can help you see your strengths and areas for improvement, offer advice based on your own experiences, and hold you accountable as you seek to grow.

Biblical Example: Paul and Timothy

The relationship between the Apostle Paul and Timothy is one of the best examples of mentorship in the Bible. Paul took Timothy under his wing, guiding him in his ministry and encouraging him to use his gifts with boldness. In 2 Timothy 1:6 (NIV), Paul writes, *"For this reason, I remind you to fan into flame the gift of God, which is in you through the laying on of my hands."* Paul's mentorship helped Timothy grow in confidence and effectiveness as a leader in the early church.

Having a mentor like Paul can help you fan into flame the gifts that God has placed within you. A mentor can provide personalized guidance and wisdom, helping you navigate challenges and grow in your gifts.

Practical Tip: Finding a Mentor

If you don't currently have a mentor, start by praying for God to bring someone into your life who can guide you spiritually. Look for someone who is spiritually mature, wise, and experienced in the areas where you want to grow. This could be a pastor, a small group leader, or a seasoned believer in your church.

Once you identify someone, don't be afraid to ask them to mentor you. Be clear about what you hope to gain from the relationship, and approach them with humility and a willingness to learn. Most mature believers will be honored to walk alongside you in your spiritual journey.

Accountability and Encouragement in Community

A key benefit of being in a supportive community and having mentors is the accountability and encouragement they provide. When you share your spiritual journey with others, you allow them to speak truth into your life, helping you stay focused on your calling and gifts. Accountability helps prevent complacency and keeps you growing.

Proverbs 27:17 (NIV) says, *"As iron sharpens iron, so one person sharpens another."* True spiritual growth happens when we allow ourselves to be sharpened by others in our community. They can point out areas where we need to improve, offer encouragement when we feel discouraged, and celebrate our victories as we step into our gifts.

Practical Example: Accountability Partners

John and Mark were two men in the same small group who both felt called to leadership within their church. They agreed to be accountability partners, regularly checking in on each other's progress and praying for each other's growth. Over time, this relationship helped them both stay motivated, face their fears, and develop their gifts of leadership and service.

Like John and Mark, finding someone to hold you accountable can help you stay committed to using your gifts. Whether it's a friend, a mentor, or a group of believers, having others invest in your journey will make all the difference.

Cultivating Authentic Relationships

To build a supportive community, it's important to cultivate authentic, intentional relationships. These relationships should be based on mutual trust, respect, and a shared commitment to spiritual growth. Authentic relationships provide a safe space to be vulnerable, ask for help, and receive encouragement.

Biblical Example: Jonathan and David's Friendship

The friendship between Jonathan and David is a beautiful example of an authentic, supportive relationship in the Bible. Despite the challenges they faced, Jonathan remained loyal to David, encouraging him in difficult times and helping him navigate his calling. In 1 Samuel 18:3-4 (NIV), we see that Jonathan made a covenant with David, showing his commitment to supporting and protecting him.

Authentic relationships, like the one between Jonathan and David, can provide the support you need to grow in your spiritual gifts. Building such relationships takes time and effort, but the rewards are invaluable.

Practical Tip: Invest in Relationships

If you don't currently have strong, supportive relationships, consider joining a small group, ministry team, or church activity where you can meet other believers. Be intentional about investing in these relationships by being vulnerable, offering encouragement, and making time to connect regularly. The more you invest in others, the more they will invest in you.

The Power of Prayer in Community

Finally, one of the most powerful ways a community can support your spiritual growth is through prayer. Praying for one another invites God's presence and guidance in your journey. When others pray for you, it strengthens your spirit, provides clarity, and invites God's power into your life.

James 5:16 (NIV) says, *"Therefore confess your sins to each other and pray for each other so that you may be healed. The prayer of a righteous person is powerful and effective."* Prayer creates a spiritual bond within the community, and God uses it to strengthen and activate our gifts.

Practical Tip: Pray Together Regularly

Make prayer a regular part of your community life. Whether it's in a small group, with a mentor, or with an accountability partner, take time to pray for one another's spiritual growth and gifts. You'll find that prayer deepens your relationships and accelerates your growth in powerful ways.

Reflection Questions:

- Who in your life encourages you to grow in your spiritual gifts? How can you invest more in those relationships?

- Are there potential mentors in your church or community who could help guide you spiritually?

- How can you build or strengthen a prayer partnership with someone who will support your spiritual growth?

Action Step:

This week, reach out to someone you trust—whether a mentor, a friend, or a fellow believer—and ask them to pray with you about your spiritual gifts. Share your journey with them, and commit to meeting regularly for encouragement and accountability.

In this chapter, we've explored the importance of building a supportive community and finding mentors for spiritual growth. The next chapter will focus on how to integrate your spiritual gifts into your daily life and ministry, allowing you to live out your purpose in every area of life.

Chapter 6

Integrating Your Spiritual Gifts into Daily Life, Ministry, and Service

Discovering and developing your spiritual gifts is a crucial step in your spiritual journey, but it's only the beginning. The real impact comes when you actively integrate those gifts into your everyday life, ministry, and service to others. Spiritual gifts are not meant to be kept in isolation or limited to specific church activities—they are designed to be used in every aspect of your life, from your home to your workplace and your community. In this chapter, we will explore how to live out your spiritual gifts in practical, everyday ways, making them a natural part of who you are and how you serve God.

Your Spiritual Gifts in Daily Life

One common misconception about spiritual gifts is that they can only be used in church settings. However, spiritual gifts are intended to be expressed in every part of your life. Whether you're interacting with family, friends, coworkers, or strangers, your spiritual gifts can be a powerful way to reflect God's love and purpose.

Biblical Example: Jesus' Ministry in Everyday Life

Throughout the Gospels, Jesus used His spiritual gifts not just in synagogues or temples but in everyday life. He healed the sick as He walked through towns, taught His disciples over meals, and shared His wisdom with people in ordinary, everyday encounters. Jesus' example shows us that our spiritual gifts can—and should—be used in the flow of daily life.

For instance, if you have the gift of encouragement, you can use it to uplift a coworker who's having a hard day. If you have the gift of hospitality, you can invite a neighbor over for dinner, showing them the love of Christ through your kindness. Spiritual gifts are not limited to formal ministry—they can be woven into the fabric of your daily interactions.

Practical Tip: Be Intentional in Your Daily Routine

To begin integrating your spiritual gifts into your daily life, start by being intentional about using them in small, everyday ways. Look for opportunities to bless and serve others, whether it's offering wisdom to a friend in need, praying for a family member, or offering your skills at work. As you actively seek out opportunities to use your gifts, you'll find that they naturally become a part of your daily routine.

Using Your Gifts in Ministry

While spiritual gifts can be used in daily life, they also play a crucial role in the context of ministry. Whether you are formally involved in church leadership or simply serving in your local church, your spiritual gifts are a key part of building up the body of Christ.

1 Corinthians 12:12 (NIV) says, *"Just as a body, though one, has many parts, but all its many parts form one body, so it is with Christ."* Each believer has a unique role to play in the church, and your spiritual gifts are essential to fulfilling that role. Whether you are called to teach, lead, serve, encourage, or evangelize, your gifts help strengthen the church and advance the kingdom of God.

Practical Example: Serving in the Church

Consider the story of Andrew, who has the gift of administration. Initially, Andrew didn't think his gift had much value in the church. However, after a conversation with his pastor, he began volunteering to help organize church events and manage logistics for different ministries. Over time, Andrew's gift of administration became an essential part of the church's operations, allowing the ministry to function more effectively and reach more people.

Like Andrew, you may have a gift that isn't always seen as "spiritual," but it is crucial for the health and growth of the church. Whether your gift is teaching, serving, or something behind the scenes like administration or help, your contribution is invaluable to the body of Christ.

Practical Tip: Find Your Place in the Ministry

If you're unsure of how to use your spiritual gifts in ministry, start by exploring different areas of service in your church. Talk to your pastor or ministry leaders about your gifts and ask where you might be able to contribute. Be open to trying new things, and trust that God will guide you to the right place where your gifts can be most effective.

3. Serving Your Community with Your Gifts

In addition to using your gifts in your church, God also calls you to use them to serve the broader community. Your spiritual gifts are a powerful way to show God's love to those outside the church and make a tangible difference in the world around you.

Matthew 5:16 (NIV) says, *"Let your light shine before others, that they may see your good deeds and glorify your Father in heaven."* When you use your gifts to serve others—whether through acts of kindness, leadership, generosity, or encouragement—you reflect the light of Christ and point people to God.

Practical Example: Community Outreach

Rachel has the gift of mercy and a deep compassion for the homeless. She decided to volunteer at a local shelter, using her gift to connect with individuals who were struggling and offering them support and encouragement. Through her service, Rachel was able to demonstrate the love of Christ practically, and many of the people she served began attending church and exploring faith for the first time.

Your gifts, like Rachel's, can be a powerful tool for outreach and service in your community. Whether it's volunteering, mentoring, or simply offering support to those in need, your spiritual gifts are meant to bless others and bring them closer to God.

Practical Tip: Look for Opportunities to Serve

To integrate your gifts into community service, start by looking for needs in your local area. Are there organizations or causes that align with your gifts? Perhaps you have the gift of leadership and could help organize a local service project. Or maybe you have the gift of healing and could volunteer at a clinic or counselling center. Be proactive in seeking out ways to serve, and trust that God will open doors for you to use your gifts in meaningful ways.

Balancing Ministry and Daily Life

While using your spiritual gifts in ministry and service is important, it's equally essential to maintain balance in your life. Many Christians struggle with the tension between serving in the church and caring for their personal and family responsibilities. However, God does not call us to neglect one area of our life for another—He calls us to live integrated, balanced lives where our spiritual gifts flow into every aspect of who we are.

Biblical Example: Jesus' Balance of Ministry and Rest

Jesus provides a powerful example of balance in ministry. While He spent much of His time teaching, healing, and serving others, He also prioritized rest, prayer, and time alone with His Father. In Mark 6:31 (NIV), Jesus says to His disciples, "Come with me by yourselves to a quiet place and get some rest." Jesus understood the importance of balance and modelled a life where ministry and personal well-being coexisted in harmony.

Practical Tip: Prioritize Rest and Reflection

To maintain balance, make sure you are regularly setting aside time for rest, reflection, and personal renewal. This might mean scheduling regular time for prayer, journaling, or simply spending time with your family and loved ones. When you take care of your personal life, you'll find that you have more energy and clarity to serve in ministry and use your gifts effectively.

Inviting the Holy Spirit into Every Area of Life

••••

ULTIMATELY, INTEGRATING your spiritual gifts into your daily life, ministry, and service requires inviting the Holy Spirit to guide and empower you. Spiritual gifts are not something we use in our strength—they are given and activated by the Holy Spirit. As you seek to live out your gifts, be intentional about relying on God's power and wisdom every step of the way.

Romans 8:14 (NIV) says, *"For those who are led by the Spirit of God are the children of God."* When you allow the Holy Spirit to lead you, He will open doors for you to use your gifts, give you the strength to serve, and help you navigate the challenges of balancing ministry and daily life.

Practical Tip: Make Prayer a Daily Habit

One of the best ways to invite the Holy Spirit into your life is through prayer. Make it a habit to pray each day, asking God to guide you as you use your gifts and to give you wisdom in how to serve others. When you stay connected to God through prayer, you'll find that your gifts naturally flow into every area of your life.

Reflection Questions:

- How can you use your spiritual gifts in your daily life, beyond formal ministry settings?
- What areas of ministry or community service align with your gifts?
- How can you find a balance between serving in ministry and maintaining personal well-being?

Action Step:

This week, choose one specific way to use your spiritual gifts in your daily life or community. Whether it's serving someone in need, volunteering, or offering your skills at work, take a step of faith to integrate your gifts into your everyday routine.

In this chapter, we've explored how to integrate your spiritual gifts into your daily life, ministry, and service. The next chapter will focus on how to maintain spiritual vitality and continue growing in your gifts as you mature in your faith.

Chapter 7

Maintaining Spiritual Vitality and Continued Growth

Discovering and activating your spiritual gifts is a powerful experience, but the journey doesn't end there. Just like all areas of spiritual life, your gifts require continual care and cultivation. As you step out in faith and use your gifts, it's vital to maintain spiritual vitality—staying connected to God, continuing to grow in your faith, and avoiding burnout. In this chapter, we will explore the importance of spiritual renewal, how to avoid common pitfalls and practical strategies for ongoing growth.

The Importance of Spiritual Renewal

Spiritual life, like physical health, requires ongoing nourishment. Spiritual renewal is key to staying connected to God and allowing the Holy Spirit to empower us. Without renewal, we risk burnout, discouragement, and even a sense of emptiness, even while using our spiritual gifts.

Biblical Example: Jesus' Rhythm of Renewal

Jesus frequently demonstrated the importance of spiritual renewal. He often withdrew to solitary places to pray, spending time alone with His Father to recharge and refocus. Luke 5:16 (NIV) says, "*But Jesus often withdrew to lonely places and prayed.*" This rhythm of renewal allowed Jesus to stay spiritually strong and connected to God's will.

Practical Tip: Create a Personal Rhythm of Renewal

Establish a regular rhythm of spiritual renewal in your daily or weekly routine. This could include morning prayers, joining a Bible study group, or setting aside time for solitude and reflection. When life gets busy, make it a priority to reconnect with God to sustain your spiritual vitality.

Avoiding Burnout

Burnout is a common challenge for those active in ministry or using their spiritual gifts. It occurs when we overextend ourselves without taking time to nurture our spiritual and emotional well-being, leading to exhaustion and frustration.

Biblical Warning: Martha's Busyness

In Luke 10:38-42, Martha's busyness led her to frustration, as she was preoccupied with preparations while her sister Mary sat at Jesus' feet. Jesus gently reminded her that "only one thing is needed," emphasizing the importance of staying connected to Him.

Practical Tip: Set Healthy Boundaries

To avoid burnout, be honest about your capacity. Don't be afraid to say "no" to commitments that may overextend you. Rest and spend time with God regularly to maintain spiritual health, even if it means stepping back from certain activities for a while.

Growing Through Challenges

Challenges are inevitable, but they can also be growth opportunities. Whether facing self-doubt, opposition, or struggles, God uses difficulties to deepen our faith and reliance on Him.

Biblical Example: Paul's Perseverance

The Apostle Paul faced many hardships but saw them as opportunities to experience God's strength. In 2 Corinthians 12:9 (NIV), God tells Paul, *"My grace is sufficient for you, for my power is made perfect in weakness."*

Practical Tip: Embrace Growth through Trials

When challenges arise, ask God for strength and wisdom. Journaling your experiences can help you process the lessons learned during difficult times. View obstacles not as roadblocks, but as opportunities to deepen your faith.

Continual Learning and Development

We grow through practice, but also through learning. God calls us to be lifelong learners, continuously deepening our understanding of His Word. This mindset is essential for maintaining spiritual vitality and using your gifts effectively.

Biblical Example: Apollos' Willingness to Learn

In Acts 18:24-28, Apollos was already knowledgeable but humbly accepted further teaching from Priscilla and Aquila, which made him even more effective in his ministry.

Practical Tip: Seek Out Opportunities for Growth

Attend conferences, read books on spiritual growth, or seek mentorship. Continually investing in personal and spiritual development will increase your effectiveness in ministry and service.

Staying Humble and Teachable

Humility is crucial for maintaining spiritual vitality. No matter how gifted we are, we must stay humble and recognize that our gifts come from God and are meant for His glory.

1 Peter 5:5-6 (NIV): *"All of you, clothe yourselves with humility toward one another, because, 'God opposes the proud but shows favor to the humble.' Humble yourselves, therefore, under God's mighty hand, that he may lift you in due time."*

Practical Tip: Stay Grounded in God's Purpose

Regularly remind yourself that your spiritual gifts are from God and are meant to serve His purposes. Focus on serving others rather than seeking recognition. Trust that God will lift you in His perfect timing.

Reflection Questions:

- What practices do you have in place for spiritual renewal? How can you create more time for refreshment and rest?
- Are there areas in your life where you're at risk of burnout? How can you set healthier boundaries to avoid exhaustion?
- How can you embrace challenges as opportunities for growth?
- What steps can you take to continue learning and developing your spiritual gifts?

Action Step:

Evaluate your current spiritual routine and identify one area where you need more renewal or balance. Take one step this week—whether setting aside time for prayer, creating healthier boundaries, or learning something new—to maintain your spiritual vitality.

In this chapter, we've explored how to maintain spiritual vitality and continue growing in your gifts. In the next chapter, we will focus on building a legacy of spiritual impact, helping others discover their gifts and passing on your wisdom to future generations.

Chapter 8

Staying Humble and Teachable

Humility is crucial for maintaining spiritual vitality. No matter how gifted we are, we must stay humble and recognize that our gifts come from God and are meant for His glory.

Building a Legacy of Spiritual Impact

As you discover, activate, and grow in your spiritual gifts, you not only enrich your own life but also create a lasting impact on those around you. The ultimate goal of your spiritual journey isn't simply personal fulfilment; it's to contribute to God's kingdom and inspire others to discover and live out their purpose. In this chapter, we'll explore how to build a legacy of spiritual impact by passing on your gifts and wisdom to the next generation, mentoring others, and helping them unlock their God-given potential.

The Power of Spiritual Legacy

Throughout the Bible, we see examples of individuals who left lasting spiritual legacies. Their faith, gifts, and actions not only impacted their generation but also inspired future generations to follow God. Leaving a spiritual legacy means passing on your gifts, experiences, and faith to others so they, too, can walk in their God-given purpose.

Biblical Example: Paul's Legacy through Timothy

The Apostle Paul exemplified the power of spiritual legacy through his mentorship of Timothy, a young leader. Paul recognized Timothy's gifts early on and invested in his spiritual growth, encouraging him to step boldly into ministry. In 2 Timothy 1:6 (NIV), Paul writes, *"For this reason, I remind you to fan into flame the gift of God, which is in you through the laying on of my hands."*

Paul's investment had a profound impact not only on Timothy but on the early church as a whole. Timothy became a key leader, pastor, and example of faith for many. Paul's legacy lives on through the lives he touched, and Timothy's gifts were fanned into flame through Paul's mentorship.

Practical Tip: Reflect on Your Spiritual Legacy

Take time to reflect on your life and the legacy you want to leave. Who are the people God has placed in your life that you can invest in spiritually? Whether it's your children, friends, or members of your church, you have the opportunity to pass on your wisdom and help others grow in their gifts.

Mentoring the Next Generation

One of the most powerful ways to build a legacy is through mentoring. Mentorship is more than just teaching; it's walking alongside someone, encouraging them, and helping them discover and activate their spiritual gifts. By mentoring others, you empower them to live out their God-given purpose and carry on the legacy of faith.

Biblical Example: Elijah and Elisha

The relationship between Elijah and Elisha beautifully illustrates mentorship. Elijah prepared Elisha to take over his prophetic ministry, allowing him to learn from his experiences and ultimately receive a double portion of Elijah's anointing. 2 Kings 2:9 (NIV) states, *"When they had crossed, Elijah said to Elisha, 'Tell me, what can I do for you before I am taken from you?' 'Let me inherit a double portion of your spirit,' Elisha replied."*

Elijah's investment in Elisha's life equipped him to carry on his ministry, resulting in even greater miracles.

Practical Tip: Seek Out a Mentee

Prayerfully consider mentoring someone in your church, family, or community. Look for individuals who may be younger in their faith or who seek guidance in discovering their spiritual gifts. You don't need to have all the answers—mentorship is about sharing your journey, listening, and offering encouragement as they walk their path.

3. Helping Others Discover Their Gifts

A fulfilling way to build a spiritual legacy is by helping others discover and activate their spiritual gifts. Many people are unaware of their God-given abilities or unsure how to use them. By guiding others in this process, you equip them to fulfil their purpose.

Biblical Example: Barnabas and Paul

Barnabas, known as "the son of encouragement," mentored Paul early in his ministry. Recognizing Paul's gifts, Barnabas took him under his wing, introducing him to the apostles and encouraging him to step into his calling. Acts 9:27 (NIV) highlights this: *"But Barnabas took him and brought him to the apostles. He told them how Saul on his journey had seen the Lord and that the Lord had spoken to him."*

Barnabas helped Paul find his place in ministry and played a crucial role in his development.

Practical Tip: Encourage Others in Their Gifts

Take time to affirm the gifts you see in others and encourage them to take steps of faith. Whether through a word of affirmation, offering opportunities to serve, or guiding someone through a spiritual gifts assessment, you can be instrumental in helping others find their calling.

Creating Opportunities for Others to Serve

As you grow in your gifts, you have the unique ability to create opportunities for others to serve and grow as well. Whether through leading a ministry, organizing service projects, or simply offering guidance, you can help others step into their God-given roles and make a meaningful impact.

Biblical Example: Moses and Joshua

Moses prepared Joshua to lead the Israelites into the Promised Land by empowering him with responsibilities. Deuteronomy 31:7-8 (NIV) states, *"Then Moses summoned Joshua and said to him in the presence of all Israel, 'Be strong and courageous, for you must go with this people into the land that the Lord swore to their ancestors to give them...'"*

Moses' legacy lived on through Joshua's leadership, who led Israel with strength and courage because of the foundation Moses laid.

Practical Tip: Offer Opportunities for Growth

If you are in a leadership position, look for ways to offer others opportunities to grow and serve in their gifts. Invite someone to co-lead a ministry, encourage them to take on a new role, or provide chances to serve that align with their gifts. By creating space for others, you help them develop their gifts and leave a lasting impact on the church and community.

Passing the Torch

Building a spiritual legacy also means recognizing when to pass the torch to the next generation. Just as Paul, Elijah, and Moses empowered their successors, we must know when to step back and allow others to lead. Passing the torch is about empowering others to continue the work God started through you.

Biblical Example: Jesus and His Disciples

Jesus spent three years preparing His disciples to carry on His ministry after His ascension. He taught, mentored, and equipped them to spread the Gospel. Matthew 28:19-20 (NIV) captures this: *"Therefore go and make disciples of all nations... teaching them to obey everything I have commanded you..."*

Jesus passed the torch to His disciples, whose obedience allowed the Gospel to spread throughout the world. His legacy continues today through those who follow Him.

Practical Tip: Empower Future Leaders

Look for opportunities to empower future leaders as you build your legacy. Whether through mentorship, guidance, or encouragement to step into leadership roles, be intentional about passing the torch. Your spiritual impact will continue through those you invest in, as God uses their gifts to carry on His work.

Reflection Questions:

- **Who in your life can you mentor or invest in spiritually?**
- **How can you help others discover and activate their spiritual gifts?**
- **Are there opportunities for you to pass the torch and empower future leaders in your church or community?**
- **What kind of spiritual legacy do you want to leave behind?**

Action Step:

THIS WEEK, IDENTIFY one person you can encourage, mentor, or help discover their spiritual gifts. Take a step of faith to invest in their spiritual growth and build a lasting legacy.

In this chapter, we've explored how to build a legacy of spiritual impact by mentoring others, passing on your gifts, and empowering future leaders. In the next and final chapter, we will reflect on the journey of discovering your spiritual gifts and offer encouragement as you continue to walk in your God-given purpose.

Chapter 9

Walking in Your God-Given Purpose

Throughout this journey of discovering and activating your spiritual gifts, you've learned about the incredible power and potential that God has placed within you. You've explored the biblical foundations of spiritual gifts, gained practical tools for identifying and nurturing your gifts, and considered how to maintain spiritual vitality. Now, as you walk in your God-given purpose, it's important to keep your eyes fixed on the One who has called you and to continue growing in faith and service.

This chapter will offer final encouragement and guidance as you continue your journey, reminding you of the joy and responsibility that comes with walking in your gifts and fulfilling your God-given calling.

Embrace Your Unique Calling

One of the most beautiful aspects of spiritual gifts is that no two believers are the same. God has uniquely designed you with gifts, talents, and experiences that are tailored to your specific purpose. The church is made up of many different parts, and each part has a role to play. 1 Corinthians 12:18 (NIV) says, *"But in fact, God has placed the parts in the body, every one of them, just as he wanted them to be."*

Your calling is not identical to anyone else's. You have a distinct role to fulfill in God's kingdom, and your gifts are a vital part of His plan. Embrace the uniqueness of your calling, knowing that God has equipped you for the exact purpose He has set before you.

Practical Example: The Beauty of Diversity in Gifts

Consider a church service where a variety of spiritual gifts are being used. The preacher is using the gift of teaching to deliver a powerful message, while the worship team is using their musical gifts to lead the congregation in praise. In the background, someone with the gift of administration is organizing the event, and others with gifts of hospitality are welcoming newcomers. Still others are quietly praying for the service, using their gift of intercession. Every person is contributing something unique, yet all are working together for the same purpose: to glorify God and build up the church.

This diversity of gifts is essential to the functioning of the body of Christ. Whatever your gifts may be, they are important and needed. By fully embracing your role and allowing others to embrace theirs, the church becomes a beautiful reflection of God's creativity and purpose.

Continue Seeking God's Guidance

Even after discovering your spiritual gifts, it's important to continue seeking God's guidance as you use them. God's plans for your life may shift and evolve, and He will continue to direct you on how to use your gifts most effectively.

Proverbs 3:5-6 (NIV) reminds us, *"Trust in the Lord with all your heart and lean not on your understanding; in all your ways submit to him, and he will make your paths straight."* As you walk in your gifts, keep your heart open to God's leading. He may open new doors, call you to new ministries, or bring you to places where your gifts will be needed in ways you never imagined.

Practical Tip: Prayer for Ongoing Guidance

Make it a regular practice to seek God's guidance in prayer. Ask Him to show you how to use your gifts each day, and be open to new opportunities that align with His will. Stay sensitive to the Holy Spirit's promptings, trusting that God will lead you to where your gifts can make the greatest impact.

Step Out in Faith

One of the most important aspects of walking in your God-given purpose is stepping out in faith. Activating your spiritual gifts may require you to move beyond your comfort zone, take risks, and trust God in new ways. Often, God's calling will lead you into situations where you feel unprepared or unqualified—but it's in those moments that God's power is made perfect in your weakness.

2 Corinthians 12:9 (NIV) reminds us of this truth: *"My grace is sufficient for you, for my power is made perfect in weakness."* When you step out in faith, relying on God's strength rather than your own, He will empower you to accomplish things far beyond your abilities.

Personal Story: Overcoming Fear to Walk in Faith

Consider the story of a believer named Rachel, who had always felt drawn to evangelism but was terrified of speaking in public. For years, she avoided sharing her faith, feeling inadequate and afraid of rejection. One day, while praying, she felt God calling her to lead a small Bible study group for new believers. Despite her fear, Rachel stepped out in faith and trusted God to give her the words to say.

As Rachel began leading the group, she saw God work through her in incredible ways. People's lives were changed, and Rachel's confidence in her gift grew. What started as a small step of faith became a powerful ministry that continues to impact others. Rachel's story is a reminder that God can use even our greatest fears to accomplish His purposes when we trust Him.

• • • •

Stay Grounded in Humility

As you continue to use your gifts, it's essential to stay grounded in humility. Spiritual gifts are not about elevating ourselves, but about serving others and bringing glory to God. 1 Peter 4:10-11 (NIV) says, *"Each of you should use whatever gift you have received to serve others, as faithful stewards of God's grace in its various forms. If anyone speaks, they should do so as one who speaks the very words of God. If anyone serves, they should do so with the strength God provides, so that in all things God may be praised through Jesus Christ."*

When you use your gifts with humility, you acknowledge that they are a gift from God, not something you've earned or achieved. This attitude keeps you focused on serving others rather than seeking personal recognition or praise.

• • • •

PRACTICAL TIP: SERVE Without Expectation of Praise

Make it a habit to serve with no expectation of recognition. Whether you're using your gifts in a visible role or behind the scenes, remind yourself that your service is for God's glory, not your own. Look for opportunities to serve others humbly, and trust that God will honor your heart of service.

Cultivate a Heart of Gratitude

Gratitude is a key component of walking in your God-given purpose. When you recognize that your gifts are a blessing from God, it cultivates a heart of thanksgiving and joy. Gratitude shifts your focus from what you don't have to what God has already given you. It helps you appreciate the unique ways God is working in and through you.

Colossians 3:17 (NIV) encourages us, *"And whatever you do, whether in word or deed, do it all in the name of the Lord Jesus, giving thanks to God the Father through him."*

Practical Tip: Journal Your Gratitude

One practical way to cultivate gratitude is by keeping a gratitude journal. Regularly write down the ways you see God working in your life, especially in how He's using your spiritual gifts. Reflect on moments when God has provided opportunities to serve, blessed you with growth, or allowed you to make a difference in someone's life. Gratitude will keep your heart aligned with God's purposes and remind you of His goodness.

Trust in God's Perfect Timing

Lastly, as you walk in your purpose, trust in God's perfect timing. Sometimes, it may feel like your gifts are not being fully used, or that your calling is not yet clear. But God is always at work, preparing you for the right time and place to use your gifts. Be patient and trust that He is shaping you for His purposes.

Ecclesiastes 3:11 (NIV) reminds us, *"He has made everything beautiful in its time."* Trust that God's timing is perfect and that He will use your gifts at exactly the right moment for His glory.

Practical Example: Trusting in God's Timing

Consider the story of Joseph in the Bible. Joseph had dreams of leadership at a young age, but it took many years—and many difficult experiences—before those dreams were realized. Yet, through every season of Joseph's life, God was preparing him for his ultimate purpose. When the time was right, Joseph stepped into his calling as a leader who saved many lives.

In the same way, trust that God is working behind the scenes, even when you don't see it. Stay faithful, continue using your gifts as opportunities arise, and know that God will reveal His perfect plan in His perfect timing.

Reflection Questions:

- What unique gifts and callings has God given you? How can you fully embrace your role in His kingdom?
- In what areas of your life do you need to step out in faith and trust God more?
- How can you cultivate a heart of humility and gratitude as you walk in your purpose?
- Are you trusting in God's perfect timing for your life and gifts? What might He be preparing you for?

Action Step:

This week, take a step of faith in using your spiritual gifts. Whether it's volunteering in a new ministry, reaching out to someone in need, or simply praying for God's guidance, trust that He will lead you as you continue walking in your God-given purpose.

This final chapter concludes your journey in discovering and activating your spiritual gifts. As you move forward, remember that your gifts are not just for your benefit but for the building up of the body of Christ. Walk boldly in your calling, serve humbly, and trust that God will continue to use you in powerful ways for His kingdom. Stay connected to Him, stay open to His leading, and continue growing in faith as you live out the purpose He has uniquely designed for you.

Conclusion

As we conclude our journey through "Gifted for Purpose: Unlocking Your Spiritual Gifts for a Fulfilling Life," it's essential to pause and reflect on the incredible adventure you've undertaken. Discovering and activating your spiritual gifts is not merely a personal endeavor; it's a divine calling that allows you to participate in God's transformative work in the world. Throughout this book, we've explored the biblical foundation of spiritual gifts, provided practical tools for identification and activation, and emphasized the importance of community and mentorship.

In this final chapter, we will summarize key takeaways, encourage ongoing growth, and inspire you to embrace your life as a gifted individual living out your purpose.

Several key themes have emerged throughout this guidebook, highlighting the importance of understanding and activating your spiritual gifts:

- Biblical Foundation: Spiritual gifts are rooted in Scripture and given by the Holy Spirit for the common good. They serve specific purposes within the body of Christ and are essential for the church's mission.

- Identifying Gifts: Through examining passages like 1 Corinthians 12, Romans 12, and Ephesians 4, you've learned about various spiritual gifts and how to recognize which ones resonate with your experiences, passions, and abilities.

- Practical Activation: You have been equipped with tools and exercises to help identify and activate your gifts. Engaging in reflection, journaling, and seeking feedback from others can illuminate the unique ways God has equipped you to serve.

- Overcoming Challenges: We've addressed common obstacles like fear and self-doubt that may hinder you from fully stepping into your gifts. Through prayer, support from others, and a focus on God's truth, you can overcome these challenges.

- Building Community: The journey of discovering and activating your spiritual gifts is best undertaken within a supportive community. By mentoring and encouraging one another, you can create an environment where everyone can thrive and use their gifts for God's glory.

As you continue on your journey, remember that discovering and activating your spiritual gifts is an ongoing process. Spiritual growth is not a destination but a lifelong commitment to learning, serving, and deepening your relationship with God.

Philippians 1:6 (NIV) offers a beautiful promise: "Being confident of this, that he who began a good work in you will carry it on to completion until the day of Christ Jesus." Trust that God is continually at work in your life, shaping you to fulfil His purposes. Embrace opportunities for growth, whether through Bible study, prayer, or involvement in ministry.

Living a gifted life means embracing the calling God has placed on your heart and using your gifts to serve others. It involves recognizing that you are part of something greater than yourself—the body of Christ—and that your unique contributions matter.

As you embrace your gifted life, consider these action steps:

- Set Goals: Identify specific ways you can use your spiritual gifts in your church, community, and relationships. Set achievable goals that allow you to step out in faith and serve others.

- Seek Opportunities: Look for opportunities to use your gifts in new and diverse settings. Volunteer for ministries that align with your gifts, and remain open to serving in unexpected ways.

- Continue Learning: Attend workshops, seminars, or classes that focus on spiritual gifts, ministry skills, or personal development. Continuous learning will equip you to grow in your gifts and serve effectively.

- Share Your Journey: Share your experiences and insights with others. By openly discussing your journey, you can encourage others to discover and activate their gifts as well.

Now is the time to take action! Don't let this journey end with the closing of this book. Embrace the adventure that lies ahead as you continue to walk in your God-given purpose. Take intentional steps to serve others, use your gifts, and build a legacy of impact.

1 Peter 4:10 (NIV) encourages us: *"Each of you should use whatever gift you have received to serve others, as faithful stewards of God's grace in its various forms."* Your gifts are meant to be shared, and by using them, you will not only bless others but also experience the fulfilment that comes from living out God's design for your life.

As we conclude, let's take a moment to pray together:

Heavenly Father, thank You for the unique gifts You have given each of us. We are grateful for Your grace and the opportunities to serve others. Help us to embrace our gifted lives, walk in our purposes, and remain open to Your guidance as we use our gifts for Your glory. May we build each other up in love and continue to grow as members of Your body. In Jesus' name, we pray. Amen.

As you close this book, remember that you are gifted for a purpose. Your journey of discovering and activating your spiritual gifts is a testament to God's love and grace in your life. Go forth, embrace your calling, and live a life that reflects the light of Christ in all you do. The world is waiting for you to shine!

Appendices

Understanding your spiritual gifts is crucial to your journey. Here are some helpful assessment tools that can guide you in identifying and clarifying your gifts.

This self-assessment tool consists of a series of statements related to various spiritual gifts. As you respond to each statement, consider how strongly you agree or disagree. At the end, you can tally your scores to see which gifts resonate most with you.

Instructions: Rate each statement on a scale from 1 (Strongly Disagree) to 5 (Strongly Agree).

Statement	Rating (1-5)
I enjoy helping others in practical ways.	
I feel a strong desire to share my faith with others.	
I am often able to discern the true motives of others.	
I love to teach and explain biblical principles.	
I find joy in praying for others.	
I thrive in organizing events and projects.	
I have a heart for the poor and marginalized.	
I enjoy providing encouragement and support to others	

- 8-15: Gifts of Service, Administration
- 16-25: Gifts of Evangelism, Teaching, Prophecy
- 26-35: Gifts of Intercession, Mercy, Encouragement
- 36-40: Gifts of Leadership, Shepherding, Hospitality

After completing the inventory, take some time to reflect on the following questions:

1. Which gifts stood out to you the most, and why do you think that is?
2. How have you seen these gifts manifest in your life so far?
3. In what specific areas can you see yourself using these gifts more intentionally in the future?

PRAYER IS AN ESSENTIAL part of discovering and activating your spiritual gifts. Here are some prayer prompts to guide you in seeking God's direction for your gifts:

1. Prayer for Clarity

"Lord, I thank You for the gifts You have given me. I ask for clarity as I seek to understand how to use them. Reveal to me the unique ways You want me to serve others. Open my eyes to the opportunities around me, and give me the courage to step out in faith."

2. Prayer for Boldness

"Father, I know that fear and self-doubt can hold me back from fully using my gifts. I ask for boldness to step out of my comfort zone. Help me to trust in Your strength and guidance as I share the gifts You have given me."

3. Prayer for Wisdom

"Lord, I seek Your wisdom as I navigate my spiritual journey. Show me the right people to connect with for mentorship and support. Help me to discern the right paths to take as I serve You and others with my gifts."

THESE APPENDICES ARE designed to provide you with practical tools, prayers, and resources to further your understanding and activation of your spiritual gifts. May you continue to grow in faith, use your gifts for God's glory, and impact the lives of those around you as you live out your unique calling. Embrace your gifted life, knowing that you have been created for purpose and designed for service.

With every step you take, remember that you are part of a larger body, each member essential for the fulfilment of God's mission on earth. Go forth, walk in your gifts, and shine brightly as a testament to God's goodness and grace!

Acknowledgements

This journey of understanding and activating spiritual gifts has been enriched by the insights of many individuals and scholars throughout history. I extend my heartfelt gratitude to pastors, theologians, and everyday believers who have generously shared their wisdom and experiences, encouraging us all to recognize the gifts that God has placed within us.

A special thanks to those who contributed their testimonies and stories, demonstrating the transformative power of activated gifts in the lives of individuals and communities. Your courage to share has inspired countless others.

Final Thoughts

As you conclude this exploration of your spiritual gifts, carry with you the understanding that you are uniquely gifted for a purpose. Your journey is just beginning, and the adventure of living out your gifts awaits you. Embrace the call to serve, grow in faith, and make a meaningful difference in the lives of others.

May God bless you abundantly as you walk in your purpose, using the gifts He has given you to bring light, hope, and love to a world in need. Go forth and fulfil your calling, knowing that you are equipped and empowered to make an eternal impact.